My W Words

Consultants

Ashley Bishop, Ed.D.
Sue Bishop, M.S.Ed.

Publishing Credits

Dona Herweck Rice, *Editor-in-Chief*

Robin Erickson, *Production Director*

Lee Aucoin, *Creative Director*

Sharon Coan, *Project Manager*

Jamey Acosta, *Editor*

Rachelle Cracchiolo, M.A.Ed., *Publisher*

Image Credits

cover Margo Harrison/Shutterstock p.2 Margo Harrison/Shutterstock; p.3 karovka/Shutterstock; p.4 T-Design/Shutterstock; p.5 D & K Kucharscy/Shutterstock; p.6 Mihai Simonia/Shutterstock; p.7 Georgios Kollidas/Shutterstock; p.8 tatniz/Shutterstock; p.9 Sergey Andrianov/Shutterstock; p.10 Potapov Alexander/Shutterstock; back cover karovka/Shutterstock

---

Teacher Created Materials

5301 Oceanus Drive
Huntington Beach, CA 92649-1030
http://www.tcmpub.com

ISBN 978-1-4333-2561-8

© 2012 Teacher Created Materials, Inc.

I see a **w**agon.

I see a **w**affle.

I see a **w**aiter.

I see a **w**orm.

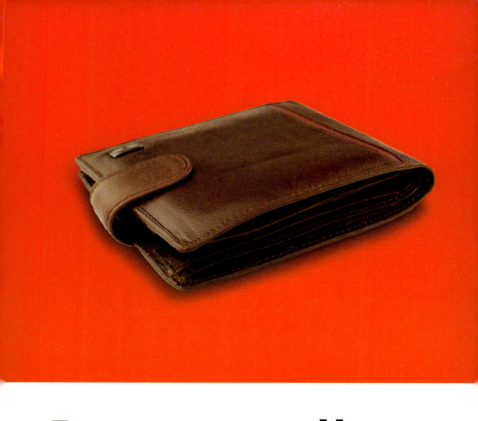

I see a **w**allet.

I see a **w**and.

I see a **w**ashing machine.

I see a **w**atch.

I see a **web**.

Glossary

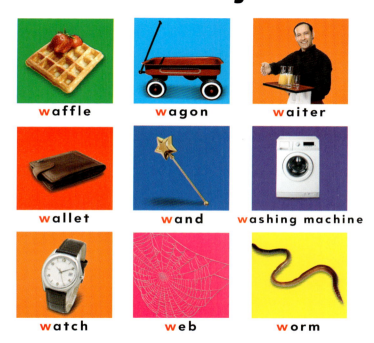

Sight Words

I   see   a

Activities

- Read the book aloud to your child, pointing to the *w* words as you read them. After reading each page, ask, "What do you see?"
- Have your child help do laundry by sorting the clothes by color. Then put the white clothes into the washing machine. Remind him or her that the words *white* and *washing* begin with the letter *w*.
- Have your child pretend to be a waiter or waitress and ask you what you would like to eat for dinner. He or she can "write" your order on a sheet of paper.
- Show your child your wallet and the different areas where you keep cards, paper money, and coins.
- Help your child think of a personally valuable word to represent the letter *w*, such as *wig.*